6 Books
In Search of a Point

Salle Hayden

Technology & Imagination Press
2008

6 Books in Search of a Point
Salle Hayden

ISBN-13: 978-0-9798991-0-2
ISBN-10: 0-9798991-0-9

First printing December 2008

This is dedicated to everyone who is on the path, and the gifts that journey can bring.

Salle, 2008

1

Book One
Loss

The Only Poem

There are so many, lost forever, now that satan's spawn has struck.
There are so many, lost to many, now that I have given up.
What is this shit that flows with ease from my fingers typing slow?
I cannot imagine so much sleeze, but I guess I let it grow.
Into my garden, I invited maggots, slugs and creeps galore.
Now I must get this pain behind me, dig for springtime like before.
I will smile and make myself joyful, because the dark and light is me.
I can only take the best now, that the muck has had it's spree.
I do know that there is darkness, with no judgment, as John has said.
I also know that I can't see it until it is slapped upside my head.
I want the green and glorious summer to come from out my seeds.
I want the world to appreciate me, and then thankfully fill MY needs.
When is it time for me to gather; when it is time for me to reap?
It won't be long now, I feel it coming; my legs are ready for the leap.
And so, my foes so few, and friends so many, this poem, the only
One for this quarter that is written, says what all said before, just lonely.

Waiting in Pain

What is it that keeps me from asking for the help
That will keep me from being crazy about those things
I cannot do right now? What is it that makes me think
That not doing those things the laundry, the bed,
The dishes makes me a bad person? What is it
That makes me think my pain, both psychological
And physical, is less valuable, less painful than that
Of others? Why do I struggle to keep up the
Appearance of being competent, when others know
How to ask for help? This makes me angry, this
Wrist that not only will not function, but keeps me
From using the other side of my body through the
Ache that permeates my heart and brain with pain.
Time is being lost to this pain. Chaos is developing
In my world because of this pain. I will not be able
To do what I "should" for the child because of this
Pain, the pain that wakes me in the night and
Sits beside me on the couch, and crouches under
My chair while I drink coffee and try to concentrate.
My life is given over to this pain that is mine and
Belongs to no other. My pain is taking over my
Life that is mine and I want to share, finally,
With others. Anger and pain now live within me,
Side by side, as I postpone my life, put my life
On hold, without pretty music to listen to now.

5

Your Voice

The clamshell phone snaps shut and
Already your words swirl between my ears,
Recounting again and again the love
We share. You are so near, here in
My heart, and oh, so far away, there,
On the other end of the line, miles and
Days away. But the echo of your spoken
Thoughts spins through my brain,
Instilling in my memory those tones
I know so well, and miss when you're
Not here. Your voice has become
A part of my soul, living in my heart,
And just below, flowing through the chi
That fills me with glowing light energy
At the start of each call, when you say
"Hello, I miss you, Darling" in your voice.

Loss

The hole, the emptiness, the sucking
Sound you hear, the cold shudder of
Fear and pain, the quiver in your belly,
This is the measure of loss. The only time
You will experience this as a tsunami,
A Katrina, a weather report after the quake
Is when the personal loss appears so
Great that nothing will ever take the place
Of what is gone. Then the mourning
Begins. Then the healing begins, but
Never until you let the entire feeling
Wring your heart dry of blood, creating
A vacuum where there once was a
Flood of love, or pleasure, or peace.

A Poem a Day

That's the promise that was made,
A poem a day for the good of the universe,
But lately it seems like these pearls
Are harder than the grains of sand
They should be growing from. They
Burn and irritate and anger me so
That they, themselves, get in the way
Of the writing, the value, the idea.

Farewell Under a Spring Full Moon

The potion's been administered, all for well and good.
The rationalizations have been stated, in no uncertain,
Well, a little uncertain, terms, and incense has burnt.
The candle is almost finished, not such a big candle,
And your body twitches with the finality of it all. Lucky,
The cat with the question mark ostrich-plume tail,
Walking away down the hall bow-legged in front
And decidedly pigeon-toed and knock-kneed at the rear,
With your crow-like voiced questions, you have been
A good companion to several of us over the years.
You didn't earn or use your mask-sneer. You never
Scowled at anyone. You gazed or were under the bed,
That's all. You finally got pretty good at giving the same
As you got from the Alpha Princess cat-like witch's pet.
Yes, sadness is sitting in the rocking chair watching the
Process, but sadness will never dwell at our hearth.
Your life was good, and you gave kisses from the heart,
To thank anyone for food, water and even one more day.
Your heart-beat has speeded up but grows faint and
Your lungs take in so little air the rise and fall must
Be felt rather than seen. The full May moon enters
Through the window and falls near your bed, with
Rays to light your way. Climb now, our pet, into the
Chariot awaiting your return to the center of the source.
It's done. You're gone and there will be no more pain,
At least, not this time around. Farewell, Lucky Star.

Desire

My skin is crawling
Into the corner & shaking
With desire for you while
I sit here, trying to hold
Myself together without
My skin. How can I go on
With so little touching?
How can I go on? Is this
One more promise broken?
Oh, I know, not on purpose
But the pain remains daily.

Sad Little Lives

All those people over there are living sad little lives.
Every year, going out and sharing
Important occasions with family, friends and
Neighbors, but what is really important about any
Occasions but birth and death?
Disasters strike, and people are swept away
By the devastation, but the shock and trauma cannot
Give meaning to their sad little lives.
Terrors in the night, fear of the future
What are those to us who are leading
Our own sad little lives? We met and the earth moved,
And we didn't even meet to move it. Our tremendous
Love is not enough to change the patterns of our own
Sad little lives. Who is unselfish now? Only the martyr
Who chooses to stay inside the box to make sure that
The children will never know how much he feels
In his sad little life. Protect the kids from knowing
That their father has a passion so great that he cannot
Contain it, and it overflows into the streets, while
Walking through this sad little life. Who is so needy now?
Only the one who must take back control, the wheel that slipped
Through her fingers as they were careening down
The garden path. And now, where will their sad little
Lives take them? Far, far away, farther than ever before,
To places that cannot be visited except in dreams,
Dreaming of the chances that must be put away,
To take out, like a souvenir, turning over in wrinkled
Fingers, remembering that there had
Been a day, when life was not sad.

Our Past

So far apart we have grown, and yet
Memory looms above, like clouds
Of mist and smoke. Dreams of you
Still drift about my room at times.
You thought me small and distant
Quite a bit before I did the same
To you. But we had the tools to
Create "us" from our thoughts.
Now that "us" goes on as we
Weave our friendship through the
Stream of time that floats above
And below. I have these feelings
Of nostalgia, as I live a different
Life, not so different really from
What I dreamt would be with you.
I wonder if your memories of me
Come back to haunt you, too,
But only in the nicest way, with
Cheek-kisses and tender hugs,
And wishes for another chance.

The Kiss That Never Was

In the airport, the first meeting, the first glance of
Eyes to eyes. Standing and staring, finally seeing
In the flesh who had been imagined for so long.
Is that disappointment that is creeping into her eyes?
Is that judgment in the bend of his head and furrowed brow?
No, just passing glances, not sure that what is seen
Is real. After so much time, so many words shared,
Who can tell being awake from the dream? Feeling clumsy,
Stepping closer now, tripping over luggage, just a little,
Reaching out with tentative hands. Right up and
Left around waist, or vice-versa? Her hands on his shoulders
And his hands on her hips. That is not enough.
Closer still, a step, an inch. Two arms encircling
His strong neck. Two arms encircling her waist.
Eyes locked. Smiles wide enough to make the dentist
Happy for the pose that will sell orthodontia to the masses.
Closer, one centimeter more, then knees are touching,
Upper bodies pushed away for the view. But now
Thighs meet and stomachs blending into one middle,
Into one vast chi of the universe. He tilts his head
A bit to the right. She does the same. Mouths meet.
Pouf! The dream is over again, as always. There is
No way to go beyond the first kiss, so why begin it?
If bodies meet and arms entangle, the beginning and
The end will all be started on one plane, and there
Will never be another time but now, the grasp, the hug,
The one vast kiss that encompasses eternity forever, now.

The New Phone Protocol

There was a day, many of them,
When we would say nothing, for a long time
And then, with an elaborate goodbye ritual,
Hang up, knowing that the next day
Would be another day. Thank you
For today. Thank you for being on the
Telephone today. Thank you for being the one
I can drink my water for; I can walk the distance for;
I can smile for, with or without wrinkles. And yet,
It's not really for the You that sits there, so far
Away, who is the purpose behind me taking care
Of me. It is still a wispy dream of who we
Could have been that is the impetus for
All my healthy living. I am living, knowing that
I have one foot in that fog, and one foot on
The solid, seen ground. Day by day,
I will be learning to inch that foggy foot
Out of the mist and into the sun,
Where, on both feet solidly planted,
I will take care of myself because I know
That I am worth it. Until that day, as they say
In Al-Anon, when I can love myself, I'll let you
Love me as you do, and I'll do good things for you.
And when the call is done, dragged out with
Something new to share, something more to say,
When that call is over, we will take many minutes to say,
"I love you. Be well" and "Goodbye."

Fur Fear

The door was locked, but wide, wide open
To the wide and wider world than she'd known.
Her wicked eyes are not watching from a
Corner this time. Her cry is not answering
Mine. I hesitate to feel the fear that creeps
Over my spine and neck. She can't be
Gone. No. Now I've said/written the word
That could make it so. To manifest
Abundance, create a vacuum, he said,
But this is too much, too much. Come
Back, little Sheba, little Princess Seadawn.

At This Moment

Had you been unwise, we would be crying,
Clinging and crying, baggage already checked
For return, you to go back to whence you came
And I to stay, trying to breathe for another day,
But crying. I know that both would be crying
At this very moment in the airport, queuing up
With boarding pass, at the gate where I cannot go,
Clinging and crying. You would not want to leave,
I would have already begun to grieve for your
Departure. Breathing would be hard for each
And both together. Or another scenario perhaps.
You would be the man of stone, already knowing
That if you did not hold your own, we would
Both be crying. So you would not, could not
Let down that barrier you have built around
Your mound of heart and mind and soul, all
Lumped together. You would be strong
For both of us, and I would be crying. But
Neither of these scenes are taking place
At this moment, because you were so afraid
And so wise to know that if you had come
Then inevitably you would have to go,
And someone would be crying on the outside
And someone would be crying on the inside
At this moment, at the airport, as we part
Again. But, at this moment, I am writing
Of the potential for crying, and celebrating
That both of us, because we know each other,
Have this potential now, at this moment, that
We did not have before. Gratitude fills my
Heart, at this moment, for this knowledge.

Kissing

Oh, how I had been missing kissing.
And now that I have kissed and been
Kissed, and know what I have missed,
It's fun, but I remember better that it's
Not as important as I made it lately.
Oh, how I had been missing hugging
And touching, but now that I have
Hugged and touched, and been
Hugged, and touched, I remember
That it's not as important as I made it
Lately. I remember that the most
Important part is the feeling of
Knowing that the person with whom
I'm sharing hugging and kissing
Is an important person in my life.
Oh, how I had been missing loving.
But now that I have found love, and
My love has been returned, I know
That the loving is the most important
Part of being alive, and I am so alive
Today because I can say, I love and
Am loved. Sure, I'll keep on kissing
And hugging and looking for another
To be loved and loving, but today
I can say, thank you to the universe.

17

The Saddest Goodbye

When things have changed, and love
Has turned its face away, no matter
The reason, there is that moment
When we must say the words that
Give pain, and pleasure, through
Finality. Because I loved you so much
And you loved me so much, our star
Was like a nova that raced across
The sky, and burned out, too quickly.
Now that we have grown apart
Because we cannot grow together
What is the task that lies before us?
I must go on and away and learn
To live another day without you.
You must say the final words before
You turn your face to another life.
Analysis shows us that the unfinished
Thing is the thing that haunts.
I know, my Love, you want no more
Analysis, but grant me this final
Observation: the saddest goodbye
Is the one that is never said.

The Essence That Is Burned

Heart and soul seem so encompassing,
And feel as though it will last forever,
When the statement is made, without
A question to preface it, "Your essence
Is burned into my heart and soul."
What can that mean? Does it mean,
For instance, that you are so changed
By knowing me that your life will forever
Be different? Can it mean that you
Have learned something new that will
Stay with you forever? Can it mean
That gratitude for gratitude, and me,
Will permeate your life, and show you
Happiness now that you missed seeing?
Or can it mean that, etched like a
Statement of fact in white words on
A black glass plaque, you are changed
And in pain from the difference? That
You wish to be free of the pain that
This burning brings you? That you
Want to forget these changes and
The statements made in dreams
Because there will never be joy in
Reality? Choices that have been made
Will live on. The door cannot be closed.
The essence will remain, in scars,
On your heart and soul, and the
Scars will fade, over time, but if you
Look carefully, you will remember.

Tasks for Today

Meditate, without thinking about him.
Take a shower, without remembering how
He spoke about soaping and rinsing
Off the soap. Make coffee at the counter
That he could see in a photo sent.
Read the newspaper, without checking
What the weather is like in Maryland
And North Carolina. Drive to class
Without talking on the phone, with anyone.
Write a poem, without him being
The subject or the impetus. Drink
Water, without reflecting on how
I'm being a good girl for him.
Check the email, without looking at
Messenger to see if he is available.
Walk, without meditating on all the
Phases of us, under the full moon
We shared. Eat dinner, to keep up
My strength, so that I can rise
And perform all of my tasks
Tomorrow, without thinking of him.

Distance & Solitude

I am a lover of being alone.
That's why I choose married men to love and be loved by.
Commitment is too much for me.
I must be abandoned in order to know that caring is beyond
My environment. Oh, don't get me wrong I care, too much,
But I cannot touch what I cannot have, and therein lies the pain.
I must be alone. I must be alone.
I must work in solitude and gain the rites of passage into my
Heart by myself. There was fear, before I learned this. The fear
That I would always be alone.
Well, here I am, and it's not so bad, being alone and finding
That my company is enough for me. I am so far from those
I love, and they are distant from me, but I do not dwell
In flesh. I am spirit, and my spirit is everywhere, with them
And with me. I cannot be the one who takes care of my lovers,
Day to day, but they know and I know that
In each and every way, we are enough for the world and
Ourselves. I am alone, but I am also the universe,
And unchanged by belonging to myself instead of another,
I can reach out and give to anyone who needs to know
That they are not alone the knowledge of connectedness.
I am distant, and alone, but I am everywhere and
At one with all.

The Biggest Loss of All

The keys where are the keys? I can't drive, or
Lock the house, or get into the office without the keys.
Where are the keys? What are you done with them?
Oh, [take a breath, Honey] they're right here. Yes,
Yes, I know I looked there and I'm sure they were not,
But now they are and that's all that matters to me.

The Bluetooth where is the Bluetooth? I don't
Want to spend more money to replace what I already
Have, even if I don't have it this minute. What have
I done with it? I'm sure it was on this counter, just
Yesterday afternoon. That's what I get for leaving
Things on the counter that are the size, shape and
Color of a small rodent. Ah, there it is [two days later],
On the floor, cat gnawed a bit, but it's here now and
That's all that matters to me. That's all that matters.

My innocence where is my innocence? I can't love
Or give or take or trust or believe or breathe without it.
Who has stolen it? Who have I let get that close and
Snatch my brain-trust, my heart-trust, my gut-trust away?
It is my own fault, I know. I bring into my life he who will
Teach me the lessons I need, and I've done it again,
But now I'm just a know-it-all, because I have nothing
Left to lose. I've lost it all, including my mind. Ah well.

23

Book Two
Gifts Received

Good Trauma

In shock. I'm walking around in shock.
I arrived, so cool and dry, and when I
Leave it is in white-hot wet remembering.
Remembering looks and leaning and
Never a touch. Remember the future,
That will carry so much more than the
Past has ever done. Love, what can that
Word mean? It is potential and meat
And so much gravy that I shall
Never again doubt my cooking skill.
I was wondering whether I would
Ever cook again, but we're cooking now,
Dear One, with gas. A quiver of arrows,
You write, that God will pull and shoot.
What God is that, this God of which you
Banter, in a poem that I touch and know
The deepest meaning of, yet fear that
This is not intended. My apologies to you.
You laugh. Your laugh carries another
Meaning to my ears. There are so
Many questions to answer that have
Not yet been asked, but there will be time
This time and even the next. It has been
Fated, this shock of mine. And, as I view
The baby's fingernail new moon of TET,
I keen in wonder at the new life that
Beckons from the wings of a stage I did not
Imagine. Yet, here you are, My Love.

Speaking in Tongues

Code-talking, fire-walking,
From another life to now,
The crypto-linguist surprises me
Because I always know his mind.
Clarity of colloquialisms, even
Straight slang, does not fall
From this mouth. But
What does emit transmits
Only purest thought, like
A Valentine Michael mind-meld,
Vulcan cultural craft of communiqué.
Falling on knees in a holy place
We speak to each other with the joy
Of recognition of kindred souls.

No Quaking Here

There's no need to fear because things have swayed differently.
There's no need for the internal pendulum to lose its core gyro.
Let this happen as it must. Let them do their worst. Just trust
That he is strong enough to hold on and you are strong enough.
Life has its bumps and throws its curves. Panic is not the answer.
Just take a breath and take the meds and hold onto your heart.
It's not so difficult to breathe, you know. Even a cat can breathe.
It's not so difficult to take care of yourself. You've been doing it
For thousands of years. Even holding on to your heart is not
Such a difficult trick when breathing right and walking right
And using your opposable thumbs. Just open your hands and
Let it fall right out of your chest into your waiting palms, and
Gently, so gently grasp the edges, the palpating, throbbing
Muscle that is your finest brain. Protect it and it will start again
To do your feeling/thinking for you. Use the right brain, now,
My dear, and do not let any vestige of fear creep up your spine.
The monkey brain at the back of your head will do fine in its
Specialty of fighting or fleeing, but now is not that time. Now is
The time for all good people to sit down and strum heartstrings
To hear the beautiful music that is your right and religion.
Just take a breath, and stroke a cat, and know that all is well,
For we are in the perfect world that we have created. Just chill.

Exercise

I walk into the room and look around.
Oh yes, I say, let's comb my hair and
Tie it up for the day. I do the task and
Then walk back to the starting point
Where I remember, listening to the
Steam building in the teakettle, that
I went to get my glasses from that room.
This house is not large, but it is big
Enough for me to walk it many times
Each day, remembering the task or
Item I went to the other end for,
Oh so many times. I guess I should
Be grateful for this aerobic forgetfulness.

An Empty Exercise

Today this long, long drive
Seemed to be for nothing, but
Accommodations have been made
Through the grace that blesses us.
And so, there will be fruit
From this tree that we care for,
To reward us for our effort.
This was not an empty exercise.
Who knows how big or how many
The buckets that will be filled by
The pears, peaches and pecans
Falling into our open hands
Our open mouths waiting
For a small perfect row of fruit.

Talking is Good

Every time we talk, I stop the crazy, spinning thoughts
That take me for a ride I don't like. Every time we talk.
Each and every time your voice, with smooth tones
And lovely words, croons to my ear, I stop the fear and
Know that everything will be all right. So thank you for
Talking with me, whenever you can, to let me know that
Those dark and heinous thoughts do not come from me,
Or you, but do come to me from the past, when talking
Was forbidden. Thank you for talking with me and
Learning how to share, so you can say "I care" and
I can hear it. Thank you for talking with me and being
Oh, so kind, bringing to my mind the knowledge that
We are meant to be together, so that we can talk.

The Button

You found the button and punched it, gently
To turn on the poem machine again.
When I was afraid that there would never again
Remit from this mind and fingers another
Piece of work to smile through, because I was and am
Full of joy daily, that was a tiny regret. I would give up
Creating out of fear, despair and other negatives
To keep this happiness within my grasp for today
And every day. But look, you found the button
And now I cannot stop. This joy is growing too big
For my heart and head. My hands must labor, a little,
To bring it to virtual paper, with virtual pen, or it will
Burst my heart. You punched the button, with a smile,
Because you know that this is something that must be done.
You don't "support" my need, you revel it in, and take
As much joy as I, not reflective, like a mirror, but
On fire, like a candle beside the portrait of the girl
Who couldn't stop writing because she couldn't.
The beckoning candle, the button pusher is
Not the reason, but incentive enough to let it go
And fill the universe with her songs.
You found the button and punched again it,
Hoping that you could shine beside, and
Knowing that she would dedicate so many
To your name, another royal companion,
Not above controlling, not below a pet,
Walking beside in parallel lives,
Just reaching over at times, as it should be,
To push the buttons of each other.

Gifts Received

Gifts can be big, like the life brought to the child,
Yet to be realized when accompanied by pain.
Gifts can be small, like five bottles from Mexico,
Coca Cola to fulfill the taste of the receiver with
What is perceived by observation with love and
Serenity of true conceptualized friendship. The
Joy of receiving can be significant, when an item
Is placed into the hands. Gratitude spills over
Into life, and such a thing as knowing that the
Receiver is loved by the giver and the universe.

Gifts from Unlikely Places

Saturn fell from nowhere and landed at my feet,
Resting behind a Midget and two Brits.
Without looking this 160 horses in the mouth,
I can tell she has enough teeth to bite off
What she can chew. Whew! What a relief
It is to find just what you need, when and
Where you hope it will be. While thinking
Of a red beam, another gleam caught my eye
And led me to the prize that we got today.
And so, we buy for my guy another Sally.
How more synchronistic could that be!
Now simple transportation has a story
That we can tell the grandkits before
The fire, of when Rollie and Willie drove
This chariot to our door and dismounted,
Turning her reins over to the new owners,
New caregivers who will get use and profit.
No, I'm not ready to prophesy, not yet,
But serendipitous stops have never
Yielded better return that this unlikely
Cutting of the middle-man deal that
Went down today. Life is grand!

Who Decides Your Treatment?

When you walk through the door of unmanageability
Who will you trust to keep you from reeling?
On the day you start to fall who will open his arms
And catch you snatch you off the floor, up
From your bottom below the snakes in the grass?
And while you're down and the people are waiting
For you to look up, we want you to sense,
Since you can't even think it, that you
Are a child of God. Look up, look up and maybe
You can remember the light that you came from
So long ago. Look up, look up and see all the
Angels who will carry you back to yourself.
Look up, look up and start to think about crawling
Then think about walking. What you think,
You can do! So, again I ask you, when you
Get here, who will you let help you and
Who will you trust to treat you well?

Manic & Depressed

The more I read about this state
The closer I feel I can relate to
Ups and downs without an answer
That left me drained. I can censure
My life so far. I've come a way
From start to current, and now I sway
With the pendulum. What a symbol!
Back & forth, thoughts in a thimble.
When I put it on my finger,
Then I know why I can't linger
On either side of the swing. I drink
A cream sherry so I can think
And sit quite still for all the play.
The perfect end to a perfect day.
Kay Redfield Jamison's words are so
Poetic. My envy has me plow a row
In my own garden. Then I want
To write this down in fancy font.

The Cave

Somewhere in Kentucky, or Ethiopia,
There is a cave below a tree. Looking
Out the mouth of the cave you see, across
The valley, sensual, old and smooth-looking
Blue & green mountains. To get to the cave
Is easy. Close your eyes, relax and take
Three magical deep breaths, then take
One more, before you walk on the stepping
Stones beneath the tree, away from the tree,
To the edge of the world, and step off.
Your foot will find the staircase carved into
Rock below, turn left, go down six giant steps,
Onto a narrow ledge, and two more careful
Steps will take you home. The cave is not
So deep, perhaps thirteen feet. Twelve only
Will let you stand tall. The width is like unto
The depth. The ceiling is nowhere higher
Than seven feet. This is a magical, rock
Carved cave, with dry walls, air that wafts
And does not blow, ventilation for the fire pit
And thick, soft pelts upon the smooth floor.
You've seen this place in dreams, and
Other lives. This cave is home for clans and
Tribes, and children at play. This cave is
Refuge for lovers and would-be lovers,
And so many others, impossible to enumerate.
This cave is the holder of the soul of the
Humans from before and those to come.

The New Phone Protocol

There was a day, many of them,
When we would say nothing, for a long time
And then, with an elaborate goodbye ritual,
Hang up, knowing that the next day
Would be another day. Thank you
For today. Thank you for being on the
Telephone today. Thank you for being the one
I can drink my water for; I can walk the distance for;
I can smile for, with or without wrinkles. And yet,
It's not really for the You that sits there, so far
Away, who is the purpose behind me taking care
Of me. It is still a wispy dream of who we
Could have been that is the impetus for
All my healthy living. I am living, knowing that
I have one foot in that fog, and one foot on
The solid, seen ground. Day by day,
I will be learning to inch that foggy foot
Out of the mist and into the sun,
Where, on both feet solidly planted,
I will take care of myself because I know
That I am worth it. Until that day, as they say
In 12 steps, when I can love myself, I'll let you
Love me as you do, and I'll do good things for you.
And when the call is done, dragged out with
Something new to share, something more to say,
When that call is over, we will take many minutes to say,
"I love you. Be well" and "Goodbye."

The Empty Space

There she goes again, the seven-year-old cat,
Climbing up, purring and nuzzling at my neck.
She's pawing at my shirt, not even knowing
What she's looking for. Now biting my button
Just like she did as a new kitten, when we were
Bonding and knowing we were each other's
Possession. It's not so cute now, though.
But what she's looking for it's not here.
She wants the comfort of her mother's teat,
And she'll never find that on my chest, neck
Or earlobe. She wants to remember what
The inner-kitten felt when it got love and
Warmth and milk and fur in the mouth.
Me, too. I want that. I want to remember
What I felt when I was loved by my mother,
And she didn't criticize me all day long.
I want to remember when I wasn't "fat and
Lazy" and I could please her with a smile.
I look for that everywhere, and accept it
In little doses, as it's always given, by the
Men I choose. But now it's time for the cat
And me to grow up and give to ourselves
What we got from an accepting mother
Once upon a time, in a fairytale, a dream.

The Message

What's this feeling? Is it competence? Is it confidence? Is it love?
As I lie in my bed, just before sleeping, this surge through my heart
Feels new, and like the oldest feeling ever had. This is the feeling
I knew before I was born, when I was still eating pancakes with Jesus
And I had not been ignored, or worse, taught to take care of others
Before I should even think of taking care of myself. Where was it,
This feeling, then that I needed it, when I couldn't even remember
How to hug myself warm? I've spent so many years, coming here
To remember what I should have known all along, like Dorothy.
My heart's desire is in my own heart, my brain is in my own head,
My shoes are on my own feet, and I can do it, no matter whatever
It might be. I'll be going places, still, and I'll be meeting people,
No doubt, and I'll be doing things and making myself happy all along
The way, because this new/old me will be with me on the path.
So, is this enough to say about it? Is this all there is? The simple
Truth that the crucifix and the clock have the same message of
Freedom? Is my simple message "Love the heck out of everything"?
This surging in my heart that makes me spring out of my bed
To write this down makes me know that this new and wonderful
Feeling, that is the oldest feeling, is my message from the One.

A Robin in a Bush

Being outside is a worthy goal, and I will achieve it.
I cannot be a couch potato any longer. I must
Breathe the air and feel the blood rushing through
My veins as I walk along, in gratitude for the way
I can walk along and sing. Will I worry if anyone
Listens? Not a bit of it. I believe that listening is
A gift they can receive from the universe through
My voice lifted in joy. And it is, you know. Life
Is good! There are cats in my world, and now
Birds abound. There are chickadees and wrens
And the robin that dwells in the bush outside my
Door sings for me whenever I ask for a song.
Every day is spring, even the coldest, wettest,
Most dreary day of winter has light and hours of
Joy. Today, for today, I will go outside and walk.
Or go outside and stand in the sun, or shade,
Or rain, and listen to the robin's voice, reminding
Me to be as good to my self as myself can be.
To be as good to my body as it is to me, that is.
There, can you hear that voice, chirping in sun
And health and youthful vigor once again? Ah,
The gifts I receive, the friends I have made,
And the place where I am is perfectly achieved.

Those Country Songs

I hear it again and again, the strain of loneliness and sorrow,
That drags along in the dead of night and sings of no tomorrow.
The "I wish you were here with me" and
    "how could you have left?"
That makes each listener connect with his or her own bereft
Life and remember the sadness that ties us all together even
More than happiness and joy can ever do. We love grieving
And wallowing in the bigger pains and aches of this life more
And more each day. We identify with the pickup, dog and gore
These songs refer to even if we drive a foreign sports car
And have a cat at home. We seem to love the country far
From the city where we dwell, and want to be inside the bar
Where we can hear the tunes of harmonica and guitar
And dance a two-step or a line dance stomp, wearing boots
And ten gallon hats, playing poker or pool with the other galoots,
And riding on the citified bull ride, or at least watching the ladies
As they bounce and fall, or don't fall. These songs refer to babies
That we've left behind, sure they do. Can't you hear it now?
"Oh, baby, I had to go, and leave you and the child." Wow,
What excuses and reasons and rationalizations the songs give
For taking away the most important parts of the life we live
And replacing them with emptiness and mistakes, or money.
I listen to these songs to learn how to live without my Honey.

Anticipation

Censorship is terrible, holding my tongue
When what I wish most is to tell you everything.
I hope, I hope, beating heart pounding against chest wall,
Trying to break free to be where you are
And communicate directly, heart to heart, beating together.
In unison, in the time of the universe,
     with lungs inhaling and exhaling
The same breath this we await with trepidation. What if?
What if we don't fit?
What if we don't gel?
What if we don't, God forbid,
Get along well?
And yet, we must.
How can I want this so much and it not be true?
Hell is only waiting, no more. I've spent my life in Hell,
Waiting to be older,
Waiting to be thinner,
Waiting to be finished
With the project at hand.
I will wait no more, damn it,
I don't have time for the waiting game.
But, self-imposed, here I sit.
Waiting again.
And in the last analysis, waiting is delicious
Because my heart beats hard
When I see your face,
When I read your name,
When I hear your voice.
I'm only waiting for the final punctuation for this sentence.
The subject and predicate are here,
In the universe, spoken into law of word.

Book Three
Treasures

Breath of Life

Weighty, lying on my chest,
Across the highest ribs that
Rest under collar bone, this
Is her nest, her resting place.
She cares not for my book or
Program. She does not look
At my face for more than a
Moment, then her gaze lifts up
As if to watch a lazy summer fly.
But now it's winter and no flies
Survive, so I know it's just her
Way of keeping me in my place.
And then I feel it upon my cheek,
The tiniest caress, flowing from
Her nostrils poised just above.
This is the thing we share, or
At least a symbol of it. This is
The breath of life, given and
Returned, from cat to woman
And out to the farthest reaches
Of space, because the moon ring
Signals that travel is good tonight.
This is the breath of life, keeping
Us balanced and growing and
On the right path. Inside us,
It is chi and outside, moonbeams.

Opening the Box

If I start the words to flow, only tip up the lid of the box,
The ideas begin to follow, over the edge and onto the
Table and onto the floor. I am Mickey Mouse in the robe
Of a sorcerer, without control of the lava words that wait
Below the surface for a tap on the top of the carton
Of their home. Okay, is that in my head somewhere?
Or is that in my heart? Will my soul will them out to
Plant in other parts, to sprout and leaf and flower and
Fruit up for a harvest of poetry and prose? Or is it the
Tips of my fingers where they reside, unconnected to
Any brain? Just hide skin, that is and flesh and
Muscle words, with no thought at all to hold them to
A logical mold. Or maybe my words come from the air
And aren't from me at all. Maybe they flow through me,
And I am plumbing as well as plumber. Oh, I think too
Much of myself. Plumber? Where did that come from?
I am not that powerful, not so much in control. Yes, I get it,
I have a "U" shaped pipe that's all for the words to
Traverse before they reach their age. And by their trip
They get my special shape and hue to color and form
The poem upon the page. The rhythms of my words
Come from the piping of my experiences, the metaphors
I've lived and died through for all these years. So,
I am an elaborate system of flow-through, like the oh, so
Romantic sewers of Paris, without, I hope, the effluence.
And as I grow the words into another form, as I exert
My influence upon the cage, some part is left inside to
Clog or be taken through on the next ride. So I tap
The lid, and turn the tap, and let the beauty go again.

A Case for Braggadocio

What hubris! To kill a cat and to equate it
With warrior ways of old. Grasping at straws
And coming up cold and short and steepled
In a chase for common knowledge that will
Not be. In this world peopled by those who lie,
Here goes I, another who will tell a tale without
A sound foundation. But what do I want here,
But cheer and a story that told over beer can
Bring grins to those around me? In truth,
My friends, I want the feeling bad part to end,
So that the story will be purer. Having been
Here before, I know that door will present itself,
But never soon enough. What is it about feelings
That scares us so much that when we feel them
We want that feeling behind? When we cannot
Feel them, we can be more kind to those caught
Up in their swirl and eddies. Is that the goal?
Be free to jetty what I know, in order to let you
Let yours flow? But back to the chutzpah of
Building a case for myself of a full menu of
All the feelings of my fellows. It's so that I may
Empha and sympa and other-thize with all.

I Rest My Case

I have this briefcase that used to be a suitcase.
In it I carried all my worries about you, child.
For a while, it needed to be set on wheels and
Pulled by those Budweiser horses, you know,
The ones with hooves as big as your hard head.
And then, I learned some tools to hack away
At the contents of my case. Little chips came
Flying off my shoulders, and there you stood,
I thought. But I was wrong. You and I are so
Different as to live in different worlds. Our words
Do not compute from one mouth to one ear.
I remember the time I said "no" to you and
You communicated forehead to forehead.
"Ouch" we said, but it didn't help us know the
Inside of the heart or mind of the elephant
Sitting in our living room. Anyway, back to
My case (since it's all about me, you tell me),
I was looking for it the other day, to check the
Contents, run an inventory on you, and
I cannot find it, child. I cannot find it, I say.
Yes, I was surprised, too. Two months,
But who's counting. This is not a case of
Waiting for the fall; this is a case of putting
Away the briefcase because it's no longer
Needed here. The courtroom is closed.

Another Variation on the Theme of Possibility

There is no reason to fear, but the fear-thing
Still jumps up and bites us in the knee.
What am I afraid of? Only of me, being me.

But no, that's the old me, only a few
Months ago, I regained the chi of me,
The power that only wants to grow.

Today there is no fear, only the
Realization that what is happening
Is real. There are no options
In the great beyond that better
Or even match, the possibilities
Of here and now.

This computer is my friend again.
No longer a refuge from my storms,
I seek the wide, wide world
And get the world in return.

With burning eyes, I know,
I am so sure that possibility is my theme
From beginning to falling on the bed
In utter exhaustion because
The limits are reached
And stretched.
Boundaries are good in what they keep away
But they also define what can stay
And who is allowed and who is out.
The boundaries of possibility
Should not be strained, but
Broken sometimes, to let the universe
Give in such abundance.

The Feather of a Canary

The feather that dropped from the tail
Of the canary, in the mine
Field of hope, and detonated
The bomb of fear into the
Explosion of isolationism
That kept me from trusting myself
Is floating back up through
The air. The song of this bird
Is sweet and clear, and even if
I say I have no expectation,
I'm lying. What else is hope
But the expectation that all
Will be well? What else is hope
But the expectation that all
Will be well? This mustard seed
Of hope that rests in my heart
Shows glimmer of life,
Sprouting a leaf and tail
To match the mine-canary
In size and shape and content.
Maybe there is no poison.
Maybe we will trust again.
Maybe vocation will match
In intensity and love can soar
Upward again. Maybe there is a
Light at the end of the tunnel
That is not yet God waiting, but
God nodding, knowing that now
Is a good time to live.
The floating feather rises on a waft
Of hope so strong that it can carry
Two of us, up and up, together.
We are light, light enough to
Sit on a feather of hope.

Shiny Things

Slanted rays beam through the window,
Glancing off the crystal prisms
On the table. There is no dust film
Dulling reflecting surfaces.
I dusted here, and there & there.

Where is the Trust?

The door opened and I knew. There was no need to question.
All the answers flew toward me, like butterflies, and landed
On my shoulders and my head. This is such a new feeling
Because I've always wondered instead of being able to sit still
And "know" that truth is coming. And now I occupy a chair
That I didn't know existed for me. My throne was always
Waiting but I couldn't even see it there, in the corner of
My world. The crown upon my head shines brightly to
The skies and beams my love and esteem on high. The
Seat upon which I sit is so comfortable that I know it was
Custom-made for me, the me of now, today, this moment.
There is no doubt or fear here. There is peace, tranquility
And sureness that doesn't strain against a leash to be free.
There is joy and elation and so much hope for a future that
I know (again that certainty that the light is shining through)
It is happening today. I wanted to taste this spice before
But thought that my will could make it so. Now I know
That will has nothing to do with confidence or grace.
This is a gift that I am finally ready to accept from the
God I have been waiting to be. So, I accept it, from me.

The Comfort Zone

There's a small warm place between us
That will nourish both as it's used to
Comfort us with music and light, and
Pounding rhythms of drums in the night.
There's a kiss that will plant the seeds
And grow into a garden with bouquet
Of colors and varieties scented with
Posy-posing flowers, all with the same
Petals, but so different, each one with
A name that cannot be spoken because
It is not known. There's a touch, so mild
It's barely felt, that conveys desire too
Deep for words to speak, yet the words
Are not needed here. There's a pressure,
Growing steadily, that returns to past
Mistakes and triumphs, intertwined with
All the moments of the Now to weave
A carpet of forever under our four feet.
There is a need, a hunger that can be
Fed here. This is a place we will sup
Again and if lucky again. But not
So many times to become bored or
Angry at what is not here. This is a
Place to rest awhile between the big
Important moments of our lives, the
Comfort Zone in which to be renewed.

The Cat That Cannot Mew

This cat has a raucous voice that is
Terrible to hear. He cries with such
A pitiable "muow-ow" for attention
And a little "mee-yowt" for love.
He will purr while waiting for the
Scritch his ears require, and
Cry to the heavens when his
Water has gone dry from raspy
Tongue and voice. His call
In the morning accompanying
His sandy tongue on arm, or
Cheek or chin, is an alarm clock
That cannot be regulated. At
Times he goes off at the very
Civilized hour of seven, but
Has been known to awaken
The entire house at five. He is
A Lucky Star, and lucky that
We love him. We love his
Hair balls on the spread, and
Cries of fear and dread when
Trash truck is coming down the
Street. And when he feels that
The empty space in the middle
Of his bowl means that he needs
Something to eat. Lucky Lucky.

Home

There is a warmth and guarded safety here.
There is a breath of life that breathes aloud.
Inhale and understand the fresh newness of
The land, the walls, the spaces between them.
There are trees, and living things moving in
And out, collecting for the winter coming, that
Will be mild and graceful as the occupants
Of this new home. Sand and rocks define
Spirit of the day. Plants in pots spread the
Forest through the rooms, growing every
Where there is a surface, drooping and
Looping and searching out the light, and
Finding the light in every little corner. This
Is a home in which we stand, a place of
Family and friends, working together to
Grace this corner of the world experience
With joy and grief, and health and pain,
And all that life can give and take. As we
Gather today, to meet, and bless this place,
Let us remember what has come before on
This land, the squirrels and deer that live
With us; the natives that gathered acorns
Long ago, the shellfish that were part of this
Ocean of life. Now there are men and women
Who join their spirits to the land and make their
Own home, a home of big and little, a home
Of life.

Scraps of Paper

Little pieces of my heart,
Spread across my world,
Scribbled in notebooks &
Carefully recorded on computers
Under forgotten names.
Matchbook covers & cookie fortunes,
Each has held a poem of
Love & pain & reconciliation,
Past fears & future joy.
Little scraps of paper
Littering my path. It's lucky
There is no fine for
Littering this way in my world.
I pull these all together
And pile them high &
Count them as one treasure,
Beside the friends & lovers
That were the reason that these
Scraps of paper exploded from
The volcano of my heart.

Ask for What You Want

Be careful what you wish for, they all caution.
Be careful, don't ask too much, is what
They mean. But that is just reverse
Of what they should say. Be careful
That you don't ask for too little. The One
Can give one answer to you; the One
Can only verify your state. When you feel
Fine, the cosmos confirms fineness. When
You feel raggedy, the cosmos will agree.
Ask for what you need, of course, my dear,
But ask for what you want, and know this, too:
Abundance is in every living thing, and
Abundance is the least that's earned by you.

I Want More of That

Out of the blue this gorgeous black man,
Hoop in his left ear, swooped down on me.
Gimme some sugar, Hon, he almost said
And stole a kiss before I pushed him away,
But I want more of that. I know his name;
I know his hometown; I know his forehead,
Scarred with one across and three down.
I know his heart. I know his heat. I know
That someday soon we will meet and I will
Be glad to have another chance because
I want more of that. It's been some time
Since I was touched and wanted more.
He seems almost too young, but I don't care.
I want more of that; I want my share.
Is he a doper, an alky, a chemical fiend?
Tell me whatever, I will not pay heed.
Maybe he's a gangster, but I don't care.
I want more of that. He says he'll call
And I hope he does. Maybe he's trouble
But maybe he's an answer to a prayer.
A black angel swooping into my life,
With his silver tongue. I want more of that.

Princess Seadawn

So, why did you give me a name you don't call me?
I know it's my attitude and your father, but
If you call me "kitty" and "Lista" (who's that, for godsakes?)
How can you expect me to turn and answer?
You know, I've been around long enough now,
You can stop calling me your "baby".
Just make sure I'm fed and watered and have clean sand
If I have to decorate your sofa, I'll do it
But don't expect more, like loyalty or love.
I know I'm beautiful. I take good care of myself.
How can you believe that my royalty can give you
Oh, I don't know somehow dignity like mine?
You really need to stop rustling newspapers
And scaring me when I'm trying to sleep,
A stretch like I do and run around some more.
You eat uninteresting food even when you're not hungry
And you don't drink enough water that you've
        mixed with some food.
You sit and creak when you get up,
And try to talk with me, when you don't get the accent.
Don't ask me for kisses when I want to bite you.
You taught me to play with your hands,
So don't complain when I do, even if there's blood.
You're such a big baby, but useful at times.
You won't even let me into the closet where my food is,
Or out the door to catch my own prey.
So don't complain when I disdain your advances.
I only need care, Dear; my thoughts are my own.

Book Four
Portals

Confusion, Again

Sometimes I don't know who you're talking to.
Are you speaking to my spirit, my emotions,
My core needy being? Are you conversing with
The mentor, the counselor, the one who speaks
About the weather, or the one who cares whether
You live in grace or not? Which "Me" are you
Addressing? Or are you undressing me in your
Mind? I wouldn't mind, you know, but how
Am I to know? And then, on the other hand,
Which you am I talking to? Am I speaking
To the lusting man, or the burning hulk of
Stinking bulk products that you think you are?
Am I singing my song into a willing ear, or
A deaf ear of one who needs a different
Kind of love? And there is that wonderment
About which wave we're surfing. Are we on
The same wavelength when it comes to
Conversing? I may be in Malibu while you
Are running a pipeline on the Great Barrier
Reef. What grief there is in talking, where
Words mean so little and bodies say too much.

What Size Am I?

Am I a little thing because I feel so small
In the place I take up in the universe?
There are so few atoms that are me and
My part of the Whole, I can't control this
Feeling of being so small. Am I just
Middle-sized because of my average waist
And average breasts and average face.
I know my hair and smile are way above
The average, but my feet are so ugly.
Doesn't this all just even out, somehow,
To middle-sized? Or am I huge, a giant
In my field? I know my talents and
My skills are grand. I know that I know
Who we are, what we all are, and sometimes
I feel vaster than thou. But in the long run,
Doesn't feeling bigger and better than
The others really make me just so small?

That Door

Close the door, but not too much.
Keep out the noise & the dust
But always leave it open a crack
So opportunity can walk right in
Without knocking.

I Can Do This

Starting today I am doing this.
Starting now, I'm going to fly.
I don't need another;
I have my own wings.
Starting today, I am free.
This is the answer
To the question I've had so long.
"Who will take care of me?"
Now the picture is clearer
And clearer, day by day.
I am lighter & more cheerful;
I am less stressed than ever.
I am fearless and growing.
I carry myself taller
And thinner
And more beautiful.
I am doing this, starting today.
I am flying with my own wings.

Candles

The water is not so hot
The water is not so deep
The vent fan distracts me
From the plan at hand.
Let the candles suck away
All my oxygen, then I'll pray
And maybe get through
With deprived brain cells,
Past the barrier of intellect.
Salle, the intelligent, who's
Not very smart.
Salle, the intelligent,
who's learning about heart
And soul. In this whole
World, where is the
Integrity that must
Exist at the core?
Touch that, dear girl,
And fly.

When the New Moon

Voices from the past come ringing through the wires
And take my heart back to the longing I once held
For truth and trust and faith. Before the moment is gone
The feeling is replaced with memories washing over,
Of betrayal and distance and abandonment. Why, oh
Why do I hold these pains so dear? Now is the time,
The time of the new moon and life beginning again,
To let go and know that what happened was not me,
But it did not happen to me, either. I called it home
To punish myself for some long forgotten sins. Now
Is the time to begin, to plant the seeds of love and
Water awake the flowers of faith and trust and truth.
Now is the time to grow in grace and blessings and
Know that abundance is an attitude and my right.
Now is the time to build the foundation for a future
Wherein I am the mistress of my fate, and know it is
Not too late to start again, even as a babe in innocence.
The new moon is the light of this dance in the garden
Of my soul and heart and essence, the beams lighting
My moonbeam paths to home again, to home again.

How Extraordinary!

There I was, just minding my own business,
When the contact came, and knocked upon my door.
There I was, not expecting anything, when
Opening that door meant more to him than I.
I didn't have anything much in mind, when
We went to lunch, but his expectations
Soared, up into the blue, beyond the ordinary,
Passed what I wanted. Actually, I was bored.
I pondered on this contract, but, in truth, I only
 Wanted to eat my spinach and oysters. Sitting
Across the table, I thought about what
I might need to give. I tried to express my
Consternation at the clauses of this pact
That I might have to sign. Dancing and dining,
That's all right, but these other amendments
What might they mean? We came to familiar
Territory, but that turned into a mistake.
I hoped this was just another friendship;
The grand tour was given, and then it began.
I gave in one inch, but he wanted a mile.
The broken connection was not near enough
To chill the heat-driven movement in his bones.
I resisted without getting rude. He drove home
His point, driving me to distraction, so I
Drove him out. Cool, cool words, no heat,
The surgeon's scalpel wielded neatly. So little
Blood, no one will know. Without a scar
It will not show. The end was this, so
Plain and fair. He left. I stayed, without
Blame or guilt or shame or silt descending
Through a broken levee. No flood of tears.
How extraordinary that I bear no negative
Critiques about myself. I am amazed.

The Deal Breaker

If he isn't taller than me, that's a deal breaker.
If he can't put dishes and laundry away, or
Keep the toilet seats clean enough to sit on,
Or pick up socks and towels from the floor,
These are some more deal breakers I abhor.
If he likes to sing in the shower, that's a plus,
If his voice is good. If his voice is not good,
Then we need a solid door, but I would never
Tell him "no more singing in the shower" 'cause
That might be his deal breaker, too. I hope
He likes to dance and knows how to do it.
If he just likes to get up and move to music
That will do, but if he's too shy to show his
Body moving in public that could be an issue.
If he likes to cook a little, that's a plus, but
He must rinse his dishes; put them in the sink.
He must either be in program or support me
In my service, and understand the language
That it makes me speak. He must make more
Money than I do, but that's so easy. He should
Drive safely, but not conservatively. He should
Know how to save money, and how to spend it.
He cannot be allergic to my kitties. Cuddling
Is a talent that he has. Kissing is a favorite
Pastime of his. Holidays with family make him
Smile. Other things will make him smile, too.
Like me, and puns, and silly things I say and do.
He'll like to jump around and make some noises
But only in the most appropriate way. He wants
To please me, but not to his detriment. He wants
To make us both happy as he can. He wants to
Work together with me building something our
Business, practice, retreat center or ashram.
He wants health for me and for himself, and
He's willing to sacrifice and suffer a bit for the
Future. But the most important point of all,
The real deal breaker is that he must love
To listen to my poetry often, with "reprise" and
"Encore" calls coming from his mouth. He must
Know that through my poems he'll know me.
And then, our connection will begin to grow.

The Seventh Step

Oh, God of my understanding, Higher Power of my fathers,
Understand my cries tonight. Hear my call to you for help.
This is the first and greatest of my defects. My character
Suffers so from independence. It was once a necessary
Evil, but today I must put away the shards of glass that my
Chrysalis has become. It is my armor and my weapon of
Self-destruction. Please, my Lord, take unto you all my
Isolation and selfish ego, never letting anyone get close
Enough to give the gift of their aid. Take this remnant of
My former life away, and give it to the leech, the louse, the flea
And vampire bat, who need to learn to not depend on others.
My second defect is so much the greater than the other.
Let me catch my breath so I may name it. I feel shame
Deep in my soul that I have claimed it for so long. Again
It is my safeguard and my burden. I can't see myself clearly
In a mirror. I see distortion and an ugly spirit, and I feel
So little that I can never be enough for You, dear Universe,
Or me, or any. Please, my God of my understanding,
(Who can that be? I'm still not sure, but my faith will move
A mustard seed and protect a mountain from a locust.
Without knowing how I know or why I know, I know that tonight
You are listening, as I am learning to listen, not to answer
But without judgment), my dearest Higher Power over all,
All I ask is that I am, and truly, surely know that I am,
Enough. When these two character defects have been
Removed, my new life will begin, and HP will be there
To help me face my fears and even help me win.

Unmet Needs

They get in the way, my unmet needs.
They even keep me from getting
What I want. In the jungle the
Giraffe & jackal live together.
In my head, they also live,
Giving the four ways to answer back
When someone speaks to me. And
Each animal can choose to speak
From inside to inside me or outside
To outside you. The giraffe's big
Heart will understand whether you or me
But the jackal will judge the situation,
Escalating and creating a problem where
No problem had been before. So, you ask,
What about these needs of mine, unmet?
Where do they fit into this jungle?
When I try to meet my needs, even
Undefined though they may be, I
Am the judging jackal, blaming self
For being needy and feeling really bad.
I must grow my heart to giraffe size,
To give trusting compassion to myself.

Someone I Want to See

What's happening here, I want to know?
A feeling has stirred that kept quiet too long.
I have this twinge of hope inside, that
Slept deep within during the dark, dark
Night of my pain. I felt abandoned,
Once again, and had no defenses to
Bring to bear against the hurt and dirty
Lies that lay inside that chrysalis there.
But something is stirring. Is it already
Spring? Is it time to stretch my wings
And fly? There is a tiny movement now
That beckons me open up my eye
And look around and feel the air
Wafting gently, like a breeze of joy
Perhaps? I look through the crack of
This wall I built, and what I see I want
To see again. This is a new feeling,
Or a reprise of a feeling from long ago.
Whatever it is, I like it and I really am
Ready for it to grow. Whether or not
This is the one; whether or not this is
The time doesn't matter as much to me
As that bit of hope that I can live with
Once again. And he teases and flirts
And makes me smile, no matter how
Tentatively, so I believe in gratitude,
No matter how diminutively it grows.

I Am

I'd write you a poem,
If I knew where I stood,
If I could think of something
That might not be wrong.
On such a short meeting
To feel so much
To care about you with such
Small hope of return.
But Earth Mother overcomes.
I shall be here.
I shan't wait for you.
I shall come to you,
To care.

The Conversation of Hope

And so we spoke again, and the call lasted hours
And as the time flew, we crawled toward each other
And the future. There is sadness and pain and
Hope. There is hope of jealousy, so there is a
Little jealousy. There is hope of love, so there
Is a little love. There is hope of sharing, so
There is sharing, even today, there is sharing.
Health, both mental and physical, is a mutual
Concern. Growth and parenting is our topic of
Conversations. Pride and hope for our children,
Thinking they may never meet. But they will.
And we will have time. "Maybe more than
Twenty years, who knows?" I know, and though
I am not turning away the best, I am desultory
In my search because I think that in five or ten
Years we will belong together in one space the
Way we hang together in this emotional place
Today. Because my life has been a wait for you,
I will wait again. Your inner strengths and
Weaknesses will work for our bond, as we build.

When the Muse Moves Me

I really need to go where the wind blows me.
When it's time to write, and the right time comes,
Then writing is the way to bang these feelings
Right out of my heart, forging them into the steel
That will hold me up in the cold, dark times.
My poems are steel girders for my life. I am the
Indians of the north, clambering over the towers
Before they have skins, constructing the framework
And hammering the rivets in. I am growing
My own life, through words. They are resting
In my soul, like nestling birds, ready to take flight
'Most any day, tremulous with fear at the height
They may attain. I am standing on the cliff
Ready to fling myself off into the blue, and
Wondering if there is something to catch me,
Some little up-drafting breeze, to lift me up
Towards the sun, where melting wax wings
Will again give an adrenaline rush, before I
Plunge into the depths once more. This is my
Dis-ease. I am above the hoards, and below.
Do I wish this transport of delight and terror
To be transformed into mere happiness and
Fear? What can I do? There is no one to
Hold the net for me. I must swing, and catch,
And hold the net for self. And as I walk the
Tightrope of my life, swinging and swaying
Above the crowds' great roar of approval
And disapproval, I find it hard to get away
From the words that are my mainstay.
Yes, I am a poet, unknown to any but a few.
My audience, being small, does not, however,
Make my creation any less. These are the
Words given unto the Universe today.
When and where the Muse will lead, I follow.

My Store

I'm taking ownership & pride
In the environment I help shape.
Each day I'm here, I get
More concerned when sales
Are slow. Each day I'm here,
I put my hand to something;
I change my view. I try
To attract the eye of the one
With money to spend. But I
Also talk with browsers,
Those who treat me like a
Curator of their own private museum.
This room is getting smaller
But I'm never bored because
I dust, I sweep, I move a napkin
Just so, to control this small
Part of my life. Hm, I wrote
That last phrase without a thought.
Is that what my store is for me?
A place to meditate on my life so far?

Love

Love, like falling leaves in Autumn,
Makes us all remember sadly
All the days of early childhood
We would return to if given chance
Through falling words from sleeper's lips
Or mother, come to capture loved ones.
As your lover lays beside you
And softly snores his dreams away
You remember only your childhood
And the lovely, passed on days,
But as he wakes, and kisses tender
Befall your lips from his
You remember only the present
And your lover's words of praise.

Book Five
Gifts to Give

Women in Business

Where is the competition? Not here.
Where is the politics of money?
Not here. Where are the false faces
And back-stabbing heroes of the
Board room? Not here.
Some of us dance like fairies
At the back of the garden, in waterfalls.
Some of us haul the heavy stones
To build the pyramids. Some of us
Design the destiny of others and
Dream to meet our match in brains
And brawn. We choose to cooperate.
We choose to support. The cynic
May see us as incestuous money,
Circulating within a tiny circle, but the
Cynic does not see the expanding
Waves we create from the center,
Our center, to the edges of the
Universe. Each of us is a resource
To the others, but each of us is
A friend to many. We are the
Women in business who carry the
Weight of our lives upon our own backs.

The Poem Within the Mirror

Gaze into your face, and see what lies within
The beauty imbedded deeply under the skin,
Vibrant pulsation with the rhythm of the universe.
You are everything that is, and more. You are
All that you can imagine, and more. You are
The tiniest quantum force and the sonic boom
Of creation every moment. Do not doubt this,
Do not doubt. You are light, brighter than the
Brightest star. You are dark, deeper than the
Black hole that threatens to overcome you daily.
You are adept, and clever, and gracious enough
To take the power that is you and create a
Greater universe because your experience
Has given value-added to all that existed before
And all that will exist after you spend your time
In this go-round. Gaze into your face, and see.

Remember Me

There is no god but god. Remember,
And address my love with love.
You must look for me in human faces
Walking down the street, sitting
On the street, I look back at you.
When you see the drooling, puking
Pain in my eyes, remember me.
When you hear my cries of fear,
Don't turn away from me.
Your disgust is not as great
As mine for my self. But, there
Are days, or hours, or moments
In which I remember myself
That I am god, and then I try
To remember that you, too, are god.
We connect through our needs,
You & I. There is no god but god.

Mental Health Issued

Insanity does run in my family.
That's right, it doesn't stroll, or creep,
Or walk right in and sit itself down.
It runs. It runs to fits of uncontrollable
Hysteria. It runs to comfort others
Showing signs of discomfort & neurosis.
It runs to euphoria when the air is clear
And springtime pollens stop the nose
Because the watery eyes see the clarity
Of personal need. Yes, this form of
Mental health was issued along with
Camouflage gear and boots and canteen,
Along with footed pjs and oatmeal bowls
And fears and insomnia and joy.
Too many diseases these days are
Family diseases, affecting others
Adversely. This does, too, affecting
The world, sending tiny shivers
Of paranoia to butterflies in Brazil.

I Am Just Me

I walk into the room and you see
Authority, but it's not true. I need
To be here, more than you, sometimes.
I walk into the room and you feel
That I am a success, because
I have never suffered your need.
I walk into the room, and you know
The teacher, the pontificator who
Needs to pop you on the head
In order to get your attention. Yeah,
I do do that, don't I? But from love.
I walk into the room and you want
Me to tell you what to do, how to
Live your life, sometimes, and other
Times you want me to shut up.
Tell me when you want to listen
And tell me when to shut up.
I carry no big stick and I have
No great authority. I am just like
You are, a human struggling to
Make it through this world with
Some knowledge of why I am here.

Poetry is So Personal

Poetry is so personal.
When I speak of a double
Chrysanthemum,
You my listener, my reader
Hear a Black-Eyed Susan.

Priestess

I jumped up, again, to stand
Upon a pedestal of my own
Choosing to preach in the
Nicest non-preaching way
About how the universe is.
The miracle is that someone listened.
In the dark is the easiest time
To tell the truth. No face in the
Mirror or mirrored in eyes
Of others. In my center,
Which is your center, too,
I know it is the truth and that
You and I are the same, with
Different experiences of
Our sameness. So there I was,
Pontificating, not listening
To myself, because when I do
I have to skew the truth into
Something new and pretty. No,
Just speaking out of the love
That is us all, I felt a need
To let the children know
That they are god not
Gods and Goddesses (that is
Separate), but of the single
Idea that is us all. I
Just want to let them know,
Then they can go from here
With a greater knowledge than
Before they met this aspect
Of their very own face.

We

We have the same face, you & I,
But we see ourselves as different.
In some ways, that is true.
We have experienced different histories
And different lovers & mothers,
And different siblings with different rivalries,
But we are from the same source
And we have the same need
To return to the center of love.
So let us touch hands and connect
Heart to heart as we walk this path.

It's All About Me

You are my creation. And you, and you, and you.
I make you up as I go along, to fit my needs.
My needs can be great at times, and so I build
Giants. But sometimes I need only a little, so
A midget will do. But in the last equation of time,
At the last moment, it all comes down to the
Same thing it's all about my needs and my
Creations, isn't it? It is it's all about me.

Slut in School

When she was in high school, and alone
In every crowd, there were so few ways
To connect. She didn't get what she needed
From her home, and was betrayed by others
Before she knew what betrayal could be.
"Love me!" was her silent cry each day
As she walked the halls between the bells
And looked for a face with a smile. Any smile
Could be the love she craved. A "Hi" could
Mean "I can love you" and so was pursued.
Her gentle nature went underground to
The basest needs of all and reaped love,
If love it could be called, from every possible
Link. Her self-esteem was an often used
Towel from phys ed, dirtied, wet and on the
Floor for all to walk on. No one picked it up,
Least of all herself, for she didn't know how
To see it lying there. It was just another
Lie, as far as she knew. How could she
Cry out so clearly, and be ignored?

There is a Standard Higher

Tonight's young man, old man, gentleman,
A kind and caring soul, could sense my
Distress over the table and, while concerned,
Wanted to get away. This distress was
Physical, to be sure, but emotional as well.
Tonight's knight wore armor dark against
A higher standard. Somewhere there is
One with whom a connection lingers and
Therefore to the rue of many all others
Must take measure beside to find if there
Is a higher standard that they can match.
Wind and tide do not bode well for one
Whose beauty rang a bell within me, but
The higher standard was not met, when
Eyes and lips came together. Our real kiss
Could not achieve the oh, most bodacious
Kiss of imagination. One who loves me
And will not say the word until he knows
That my caring can be true, does not this
Standard meet. Thus far, no one met can
Meet this higher standard set by that one,
Thus far unmet, who holds the banner
High. The bar of the one who can give
My needs surcease is set so high because
I will not accept less than I have had before
Though never yet had but in that reverie
Achieved through breath exchanged in air.
There is a higher standard that, if not met,
Will still be held, even if to wait will be my fate.

Listen

When she says she wants to use the tub,
Un-pile the boxes and let her.
When she says she wants to wait a while,
Give her a chance to lose the weight
Before you buy the clothes that
Might not fit. When she says she wants
To spend some time with you and her boys
Together, building a future, no matter
How long, make that a priority in your life
Too. When she asks you what can you
Possibly mean to have her traveling
With your friend, answer the question
From your heart not from your head.
For five years she has been fearful.
Can you hear that? Can you hear that?
For more than a year she hasn't known
Who you are or what you might do.
You have been so afraid to be
In the picture that the picture really
Doesn't include you now. Do you know
How long it takes to rebuild trust?
Listen to what she says and you will
Hear how long it takes. You really must
Listen.

To Finish

There is no completion like a poem
Full-blown from heart to virtual paper,
Especially when it is a work of work.
There is no feeling like the satisfaction
Of knowing that another baby is born
And now the mother can rest. But,
When the poem does not come forth
So easily, and there is labor to it,
Keeping the mother from sleeping
Or pursuing other interests, growing
Still in gestation this belly-full of
Words can make a mother groan.
The epic poem, even the epic of the
Soul, no social commentary or
Political satire included, can still be
This kind of wrenched and wretched
Labor of love, over days and nights
Of building the foundation and tricking
Out the tiny details to make the sounds
So perfect, clicking off the tongue.

The Teacher Comes When the Student is Ready

There is a young man who wants to know the world
That he has never entered yet, and he calls upon
The teacher for support. He is full of fear that he
Will not know what to do, will not be able to refrain
From building and exploding. This is not a simple
Thing, this act of showing love and need. There are
Complex formulae and life experiences and more
That can be taught. But, the woman asks herself,
Is this who I am, a teacher of occult and hidden
Arts and magic? Is this to be my job, my life?

As we define ourselves each day, as the day is
Newly created by us, we can choose which path
To take, which fork to use, which thought to
Think. The teacher can decide the questions
In the future, not today. This is a question coming
Out of the woodwork once again, but first a
Smile to start the day, knowing that it is not yet.

Flashes of the Light

Lately I've been standing up for myself.
And I keep it a secret; you don't even know.
When I'm listening to something that's crap
I don't let my silence confirm that it's fact.
But these tiny, infinitesimal bursts of light
Are so brief you can't see how awfully bright
They are to me.
I like this feeling of feeling my feelings,
Taking care of myself when I know that you're not.
And later, I hold this idea in my cupped hand
And treasure the memory like a favorite snapshot.
I love you so much, but I'm starting to love me
And I refuse to let myself be thought less
By you or by me. So, by these moments I bless
Us both in our growth, apart & together.
Someday we can rewire the paradigm of fear
That we inhabit to include trust and joy
And Peace. Someday we will I predict
Look back over the years and be glad
That our pasts led us to meet and join,
Not at the hip, but the hand, with greeting
Each other, and sometimes a hug.
I can live with less and you can
Live with more and me without fear.

Anti-Depressant

Today, I am not upset or low
But who knows how I will be
Tomorrow. What causes these
Changes in me? I claim that they
Are automatic, outside of my
Control, but are they? Let me try
To apply my own guidance system.
I will believe that I am part of
Everything that is; I will believe
In my own abundance and joy.
I will know that I am enough,
And have a significant contribution
To make. And I will make it.
In order to know these things, I will
Take the anti-depressants that
Will keep me balanced and sane.

Book Six
Heart Beats

Doubting John

Little flickers of light, like matches
At least a mile away, there are doubts.
Moths, come to the closet to search for
Real wool, not these synthetics that
Do not satisfy, they flitter around and
Leave. These do not qualify to be
Called thoughts, these teeny moments
Of not sureness. The rest of the time
Is a sail on a clear, china-blue sea,
With no wind to flutter the waves,
But wind enough for sails to billow
And take us on this new adventure.
Most of the time is reminiscing on
The future's future, when memories
Are set and the plaster is dry so that
Fingerprints need dusting, and do not
Make imprints to feel. In this place,
That is no where but my brain, I think
Of what is happening now, and the
Surprise of finding right at my nose
The treasures of a Kansas plain, with
Friends to share the pleasures, and
I am amazed that my home is the
Place that no place is like. I click
My ruby-slippered heels and close
My eyes, and whisper, "Give me
The wisdom to know the difference."
When I open my eyes, you're still
Here. There is so little room in this
World for doubting John, my John.

Time and Time Again

Time is not my friend. It ticks and tocks
Against my brain-pan, keeping me from
Breathing, and staying in the now. I cannot
Say how terribly time treats me. I cannot
Tell how time has misused me. Time is
Not my friend. Sticks and clocks bang
Up beside my temple, and threaten to
Unseat me from the precarious position
I find myself. Watching minutes crawling by,
I am aware of why I am abused by time.
Time is not my friend. It nicks and mocks
Me as I wait, knowing as I know there
Was never a beginning, and will never be
An end to this rocking, socking, ticking and
Tocking that beats against my mind, ready
To knock me off the beam I am traversing.
And in my head I know, time is only pretense,
To ebb and flow through the terrible tides
That bring us up and bring us down. But
Time is not my friend. Internal or eternal,
Growing or rotting, changing or static,
Beginning or ending, time is not my friend.

Shivers

Again, your voice reverberates
Inside my brain pan & my heart,
Sending a quiver down my spine
To my tailbone chakra
Where it sits & vibrates,
Resonating with my soul.
Across my shoulders I feel
Gooseflesh waves, a tsunami
Of you, washing over my core,
Making ripples outward bound
To make the whole world
Know & feel my shivers.

In the Middle of the Night

The clock has already struck twelve, and my eyes can't blink.
I sit and try not to think, but wheels spin and gerbils run
Making my time twirl and dance upon the ice of my mind.
This is an Olympic performance, world class even, how
The thoughts are twisting and tripping along the edge of
My skates, gliding over the ice in figure eights and nines
And tens and dozens more. Reflecting on the glass bird
Caught in my paperweight, in a perpetual quest for nectar
From the flower into which its needle beak has dipped,
I, too, am forever on a path that leads me from empty
Treasure chest to safe to safety net from which I cannot
Escape. Trapped again in this sticky web of thoughts,
Waiting for the super spider of the grand thought of
My miniscule self, that lie I heard and believed so long
That it dwells within my heart, like a worm, waiting to
Raise its head and tease the early bird, fluttering over
The ground, waiting for the sun to rise, like I do, so often
In the middle of the night, as I mark the days until
You will be home again. Until that homecoming, I will
Sit and think and wallow and drink and watch TV and
Wait.

Summer Solstice

The sun will rise on summer.
The full moon set on spring.
Electric change zaps the air
All around. We cannot feel it.
We are it. Our status is not static
But our hair stands on end
And we can hear the lightning
And see the thunder within.
Premises of life, our agreements
Are promise of life and we
Feel it, coursing through our veins.
Stand and feel it.
Sit down and feel it.
Lie down and feel it.
Too much action around us
To stay still too long.
Get up and sing in
A wonderful new day.

Hope Springs

Hope Springs eternal, what a lovely thought.
Bubbling up from the center, flavored to meet my need
The spring of Hope will last forever. Come today
And drink your depth. No need to fret in worry or strife,
Bring your thirst to this spring and night of despair turns
To sunrise of the new day that is the first day
Of forever. Sounds like a place in Colorado,
But Colorado could never entertain
The flocking tourists who will come
To this place, this new Lourdes, to heal,
Sooth souls and beg for respite and relief.
Wade in the Hope Springs and everything
Mundane will slip away as if your feet
Are Teflon. Wash your face in the cooling waters
And come away refreshed and more beautiful
Than before. But lave your hands in Hope Springs
And all sins are washed away, shoplifting, rape and
Cruel, cruel taunts, death and mayhem will be solved
As problems mathematical, and then the board erased
For another day. Should you wonder how it tastes,
Don't fear, there is no punishment here, only the
Love that creation promised and promises every day.
This is the sweetest taste of life, better than kissing the tummy
Of a freshly laundered babe, better than butterscotch swirls
In French vanilla ice cream made at home, better than the smell
Of fresh bread wafting through the air, tingling your nares
With promise of hot butter melting soon, perhaps to drip
Over chin and chest. This is a taste and smell better than
The freshest rose, untroubled by the aphids' bite. Here
Are the hopes to crown creation with tiny, floating atoms of
The best of the One and the best of the pieces of the One.
Hope is where all can reunite in the perfection that is the right
Of all. Hope is where we come to pray, then move away renewed.
Hope is the location in our hearts of health, perfect health and growth.
Hope Springs, come and taste eternity today.

111

This Realization Just Hit Me

Now that I know, really know,
That I can be alone, and be okay,
I don't have to prove that anymore,
So I can join together in a different way.
I shall not submerge the self I'm beginning to see.
I will continue to be the best of me
And share that with the world
And another. Thank god,
Whose finger stirs my world
And guides me to fulfillment.
Thank god, who is waiting for me
To become my dream of self.
The god in me will greet the god in him
And what is dancing around the edges now
Will come to fruition in the knowing
That we already know, and
Are maybe anxious about it
Because the phone line is not
Conducive to the here-and-now and
Leads us to remember past
Learning opportunities with trepidation
And step into the future to face the fear.
This realization just hit me that
There is no fear within me.
And that which dances around my feet
Is silly and insignificant. Why allow
The past to do anything other than lead us
Toward the merging of our two into
Another manifestation of the
Magnificent One?

Too Long

My hands are aching from not touching keys in the same way.
My mind needs stretching to bring it along the quay, in from sailing
Far out to sea, not caring about direction or storm. Now is the
Time for thinking about the rhythm of my heart and drumming,
Thrumming along with the rhythms of the earth and skies and
Moon, and letting the waves carry me home. Home and back
To the way of dreaming words out of my brain and onto paper.
Too long, my life has been turned in other directions, with worry
And fears for others, not hearing the stillness inside that can
Speak to me of greater lives and bigger events than this
Small life and these small happenings. Too long have I spent
Energy on the mundane without letting myself swirl upwards
Into the divine. Too long have I been away from bringing my
Own brand of rhyme into the universe with blessing and humility.

Energy

Life force, being fluid, ebbs & flows.
Our tide is controlled by an
Inner moon, drawing & rejecting
All emotions as they come & go.
But, my Love, can't you see
That your reactions mean that
You are "out of control" and
"Unmanageable" unless, of course,
You are in control and manage
To create your world's flow & ebb
Without letting others be your moon?
The light from which we flow,
And the dark as well it seems,
Gives us so much choice in
How to draft our dreams. Do not
Allow a brother, big or other,
To "watch" you think your way
To peace. Walk there alone,
Under your own power &
Breaking your own path through
This jungle we've been dumped in.
Don't waste your energy, no
Matter how limitless. Don't
Deplete yourself to another's will
Or won't. Be strong & serene to win.

Night Walk

It's hard taking a cat for a walk.
Especially a housecat that's never been out.
It's hard taking a cat for a walk,
Even under a waning moon, because
The airplane drone is scary, and
The motorcycle roar is scary, and
The car, coming around the corner,
So stealthily, has scary headlights that
Make her eyes bright green.
It's hard taking a cat for a walk.
There are too many shadows leaning
Toward the walker, tightly clasping the cat,
Picking claws oh, so gently from the
Sweater, and grasping the collar, knowing
That, if she wanted to bolt, the walker
Would be left with a collar with tufts
Of fur, and a hissing, yowling cat
Running off into the night.
It's hard taking a cat for a walk.
There's always the chance that
You will return alone. But the
Hardest part is returning to the
Dark house, knowing that no one
Waits up for a person walking a cat.

Nothing

I can sit here all day, doing nothing.
I like the feeling of not producing, or do I?
I am producing, thoughts are flowing through
And some are even captured and written down
Like the first poem was written, before there was
A thought to spur it into being.
I can sit here all day, seeing nothing.
I like the feeling of not watching, or do I?
I am watching, images are flowing through
And some are even captured by camera or pen
Like the first painting was drawn, before there was
An image to spur it into being.
I can sit here all day, hearing nothing.
I like the feeling of not listening, or do I?
I am listening, internal voice is flowing down
Like the mother's voice speaking, before there was
A child to spur it into being.
I can sit here all day, tasting nothing.
I like the feeling of not eating, or do I?
I am eating, nourishment flowing through
Until there's no nurture left, before there was
A need to spur it into being.
I can sit here all day, touching nothing.
I like the feeling of not touching, or do I?
I am touching, thoughts become poems flowing
Through the brain to fingers, before there was
A birth to spur them into being.

The Rap

It's a syncopated beat
With ultimate stress
Making each line neat.
We can't have no mess
The bouncing knees and toes
The baggy pants hanging
Down over hips low
The drum keeps on banging.
Ideas are so easy.
It's not brainy work,
Sometimes a little sleazy
Another word for "jerk"
The subject's really homey,
Talkin' 'bout the hood.
The story's not no phony.
Reality's so good.
But then they go get scummy,
Scratch the record here, Boy.
Sex is oh so yummy,
Just bleepin' with a toy.
Don't call no ladies "ho" now,
Don't talk about your bitch.
Do negativity no how.
That's the biggest hitch.
I like the sound and rhythm.
I ain't no oldster nerd.
I wanna shout out with 'em.
I just don't like the words.

Serious Jazz

Jazz cool jazz at the carwash,
On a hot, hot day. Noise
Against music play a
Cacophony through the open door.
"Where is the civic conscience?"
asks a customer who buys while waiting,
feeling guilty about using our
corporate air. Her electricity
is off. Just the concept of using so much electricity
is off. What? Global warming?
It is not happening, some
Politicians cry. Soon, too soon,
They'll be crying a different tune.
But as for me, now it's marimba &
Latin rhythms, horns & all,
That make this slow, hot, hot
Afternoon creep on. The day drags
Its feet, perhaps, but every
Thing is slowest before it's over.

The Cat Who Loves the Man Who Doesn't Return It

She waits for him at the door, doglike,
Then becomes a cat again, aloof.
When someone wants to pet her, she flinches
And pulls away as if static electricity stings.
But when she wants affection, watch out
She doesn't ask permission, just climbs up
And kneads with needle claws for her comfort
And settles down in the worst way on his
Vulnerable lap. Hoo-boy, when she leaves
She pushes off with jaguar legs, digging in for height
And leaps across the room,
But he grabs pain
And wishes she didn't love him
Quite so much.

The Mammogram

Waiting, in a waiting room,
Nervous energy taps my toes.
Waiting, meditating on the
Changing colors of a tree outside.

Waiting, while my restless mind
Gets in the way of mindfulness.
Thinking this and thinking that.
Confetti thoughts slowly spinning down
Smoky thoughts insinuate
Into the brain & lungs & gut.
Waiting to find out
What I really don't want to know.
What does this lump mean?
What about that?

Dropped BB thoughts,
Bouncing dangerously around my feet.
Be careful where you step
Take a breath, and then release it
Jacks ball thought, bigger than the rest.

Waiting, in the ante-room in a
Three arm-holed hospital gown,
For conjoined twins?
Would they have three breasts or
Four to worry about?

Waiting, waiting, waiting.

Men with Sticks and Hands

This is a study of obsession on the quantum level.
This is a study of the DNA that beats to the beat
Of the men I have known who create the beats
That speak to me at that deepest level of connect.
This is the transition of "need" to "want" to "take it
Or leave it" to "we are one anyway, so why fight it?"
Dizzy, spinning changes are happening right now,
Today, as I write these words. The need that
Governed my childhood and youth disappeared
One day only this year. The want replacing hunger
Evolved into knowledge of my place in the universe
Only weeks ago. This attitude of "I vant to be alone"
Is, this very minute, being replaced with knowing
That I am alone, because I am the universe, and
I will never be alone because you are the universe,
Too. Yes, you and you and you, my lovers and
Friends of my life, growing within the circle of me
Which is expanding as we speak to each other
And of each other. Can't you feel it, Brother?
Don't you also know, as I do, that with sticks and
Hands we touch the drums that are our souls
Across the great divide? Can't we scratch the
Surface that is not apart, and graze the edges
That do not define? Can you follow me to this
Place of cell division, and merge again into that
Whole that we are? There are so many that
Dwell within creation, this cosmos that we drive.
We are the stars, my friends and lovers. We are
The dust of the new and old creation eternally.

Drums & Drummers

Jazz, rock and roll, tympani and taiko,
    percussion breathes at 60 beats per minute
Or dances at 97 or leaves me breathless at 120 beats.
Congo, bongos, steelhead and tambourine, rap me a rat-a-tat-tat or
Thrum me with the bass line,
    Bah boom, bah boom, bah boom, boom.
Cymbals swish, swish, swish under brushes
    and sing out from stick taps.
Snares will vibrate with marchers on the field
    keeping the brass in line.
High-stepping majors and majorettes listen for the beat,
Not the trilling flutter of piccolo or even oompah-oompah of the tuba.
It's the bass drum that calls for the batons to fly
Left, right, left, right, turn to the right,
    spin and twirl, catch and bow, step left.

*****

Before there was an Oriental orientation
    the beating of the drums called me home.
In jungle movies, the talking drums and I held conversations
    before I knew my calling.
In westerns, the log-drums and tom-toms
    told me more than cowboys ever knew.
Tabla and Beatles ragas...this was right with me
    before there was Zen or Hindus.
So when I discovered taiko in my world...
    when my world had shifted...I wasn't surprised.
I was just grateful to know that
    my heart had another beat to call its own.

*****

(More)

After years of searching out those huge-drum Japanese performers,
    when I was leaving they came to me.
On the station platform, he was tugging on my arm to go
    ("We're late.") but I was not easily swayed from
    my swaying Cobra trance to this pounding
    syncopated music of my soul.
Drummers are my charmers and I spread my hood
    and undulate as the beat creates within me
    a pulsing of the blood that I feel throughout my universe.

*****

One day on a hometown station platform, I met an exotic man
    with carved djemba, and
I felt the energy of his drum
    while he misunderstood mine resounding through his world.
He wanted more than I could give, but we took advantage of each other
Because the beat was in both hearts for different reasons.
Irish dance requires those bodhran be in tune with flashing feet. It fits
The world that I inhabit,
    even when I cannot understand the world they dazzle.
And now the Irish drummer thrums in my world
    as friend, friend, friend.
The gratitude I feel for this find resonates
    every day in every way,
    another silver thread.

*****

(More)

123

I watch any drummer's sticks, transfixed,
     and smile on cue to let him know that I am with him.
I stand below the platform and
     feel the beating against eardrum and my casing,
Throbbing along with the big drums,
     vibrating my own skin, drawn tight over bones
That no longer exist only to connect those muscles.
     The calcium of my body now is
A framework holding my own instrument
     beating, beating, beating along
With those drums, as my most sensitive heart
     adjusts to the tah-tap rim-shot,
Swish-swish cymbal, jingly tambourine,
     boom-thrum of kettle, snippy snap of snares.
All my life medicine drums have played
     to keep my energy flaring fine above the air.

*****

This is my cause, the drumming of my soul,
     comes through the words that play
Against the astral ear.
This is my single wave of the Big Bang of the universe.
Even now,
the drummers of my life throb through me to eternity,
through me to eternity.

Women in Business (page 85)
was previously printed in Women's Connection Quarterly Magazine

The Mammogram (page 120)
was previously printed in the Kaiser Nurses Newsletter

Cover design: Scott Hayden
www.haydencreative.com
Back cover photo: Ramona
www.ramonasphotodesign.com

www.ingramcontent.com/pod-product-compliance
Lightning Source LLC
Chambersburg PA
CBHW052112090426
42741CB00009B/1778